A History of

Britain

Through Art

941
P

Jillian Powell

Thomson Learning

New York

Books in this series

A History of Britain through Art

A History of France through Art

A History of Italy through Art

A History of the United States through Art

Cover: *King Richard* II by an unknown artist. This painting is in Westminster Abbey, London.
Title page: *The Battle of Britain, August to October*, 1940 by Paul Nash

First published in the United States in 1996 by Thomson Learning
New York, NY

First published in Great Britain in 1995 by Wayland (Publishers) Limited

U.S. copyright © 1996 Thomson Learning

U.K. copyright © 1995 Wayland (Publishers) Limited

Library of Congress Cataloging in Publication Data

Powell, Jillian.
    A history of Britain through art / Jillian Powell.
        p.   cm.—(History through art)
    Includes bibliographical references (p.   ) and index.
    Summary: History of Great Britain from the arrival of the Celtic
peoples approximately three thousand years ago to the present day,
illustrated with works of art.
    ISBN 1-56847-440-7
    1. Great Britain—History—Pictorial works—Juvenile literature.
2. Great Britain in art—Juvenile literature. 3. Great Britain in art.
[1. Great Britain—History.] I. Title. II. Series: History through art (New
York, N.Y.).
DA32.3.P69   1996
941—dc20   95-40608

Printed in Italy

Acknowledgments
The Publishers would like to thank the following for allowing their pictures to be reproduced in this book:
Ancient Art and Architecture Collection 6, 8, 13; Bridgeman Art Library *title page*, 5, 19, 21, 24-25; Giraudon 27, 28, 29, 30, 37,
39, 40, 44; Michael Holford *cover*, 7, 9, 10-11, 12, 13, 23; Imperial War Museum 43; Tony Stone Worldwide/D. McNicoll 4/R.
Todd 32; Visual Arts Library 17, 33; Wayland Picture Library/Scottish National Gallery 22/National Maritime Museum 35; Yale
University 34. The following works are reproduced by kind permission of the copyright holders; © Mrs. Anne Patterson
Returning to the Trenches by C.R.W. Nevinson; © Imperial War Museum *Battle of Britain, August to October*, 1940 by Paul Nash.
© Estate of Ceri Richards *Panoramic View of London in Five Panels* by Ceri Richards.

CONTENTS

The pictures in this book span thousands of years of British history—from the earliest tribespeople thousands of years ago to the present day. The works of the different artists in this book have been chosen to portray some of the major events and experiences that have shaped the history of Britain.

THE EARLIEST BRITONS

People may have been living in Britain for as long as 500,000 years. The earliest evidence of these people is stone and bone tools and weapons that date from Paleolithic (Old Stone Age) times.

The earliest Britons were hunter-gatherers, who lived by hunting animals and gathering fruits, berries, and edible roots. Some of their tools and weapons, carved from stone or bone, have been found in underground caves, where the people lived.

At the end of the last Ice Age, about 13,000 years ago, warmer weather melted the ice sheets that covered much of Britain. By 6000 B.C., the English Channel had formed, separating Britain from the continent of Europe. People began to come in boats from Scandinavia, settling in huts beside lakes and streams.

The White Horse of Uffington
This animal landmark in Oxfordshire is believed to have been created by tribespeople more than two thousand years ago, probably to mark their territory. It is thought that they carved the horse from the hillside, then filled in the shape with chalk.

Around 4000 B.C., new settlers arrived from Europe. They lived in camps protected by deep ditches and high banks. They raised animals, farmed crops, and were skilled at carving stone and making clay pottery. After about 3000 B.C., they began building large circular enclosures called henges. These were large areas of flat ground surrounded by ditches and high banks. They were probably places where local communities would meet to worship their gods.

After about 800 B.C., Celtic people from the continent began to settle in Britain, spreading as far as Scotland, Ireland, Wales, and Cornwall. The Celts were skilled warriors, farmers, and craftspeople. They built hill forts protected by banks, ditches, and wooden walls to defend themselves against enemy tribes, and they lived in huts built of stone or wattle and daub. They cleared and farmed the land using plows drawn by oxen and raised sheep, cattle, and pigs. The women made pots, ground corn, and wove cloth, which they dyed with the juice of berries. The Celts were skilled in working with iron, bronze, gold, and wood. They traded with other peoples, and they minted the first coins in Britain.

The earliest examples of Celtic art in Britain date from about 300 B.C. The Celtic priests, called Druids, worshiped gods who were believed to live in rivers, streams, and woods. The bronze figure (right) represents the Celtic smith god, whose name was Wayland.

Wayland, the Celtic smith god
This figure, found in Northumbria, was made in bronze by a Celtic craftsperson around A.D. 200 to 300. It is in the Museum of Antiquities, Newcastle-on-Tyne, England.

ROMAN BRITAIN

In 55 B.C. Roman general Julius Caesar invaded Britain, but he and his army did not stay long. In A.D. 43 Emperor Claudius came with his army. He conquered the British tribes, and Britain became part of the Roman Empire. The Romans stayed in Britain until A.D. 410.

Statue of Queen Boudicca
This statue was made in the nineteenth century by the sculptor Thomas Thornycroft. It stands beside the Thames River at the foot of Westminster Bridge in London, and faces the Houses of Parliament. The queen is shown in her war chariot, urging her followers to fight.

When the Romans arrived, they found a wild, fierce people, who painted their bodies blue with woad (a plant dye) and worshiped primitive gods. Some British tribes fought the Romans. In East Anglia, Boudicca, Queen of the Iceni tribe, led a rebellion. But although her followers fought bravely, the Roman soldiers defeated the Iceni, and Boudicca killed herself by drinking poison.

The Romans introduced their own laws, religion, and the Latin language into Britain. They built towns and forts, then roads to link the forts to the towns. One of the forts was Verulamium (present-day St. Albans), north of London, where many artifacts have been found. The Romans also built temples, theaters, and public baths.

In A.D. 122 Emperor Hadrian had a stone wall built in northern England. It stretched from the Tyne River in the east to the Solway Firth in the west. Hadrian's wall was 20 feet high and nearly 74 miles long. It was built to keep the rebellious tribes of Picts and Scots out of England.

The Romans improved agriculture, mining, pottery, and cloth making. Lead, iron, gold, and corn were sent from Britain to Rome, and goods were brought in from all over the Empire, including pottery from France, barrels of wine from Germany, marble from Italy, and jewels from Egypt.

In A.D. 313 Emperor Constantine became a Christian, and the first churches began to be built in Britain. The Romans began to leave Britain in A.D. 407 because soldiers were needed in Roman Gaul, which was under attack from barbarian tribes from the East. Other tribes from the continent, including Saxons, then invaded Britain.

A Roman Mosaic

This mosaic, made from many small colored stones, shows a picture of a Roman sea god. It was made about A.D. 160 to decorate a sidewalk at the Roman fort of Verulamium, in Hertfordshire, north of London.

ANGLO-SAXONS AND VIKINGS

During the fifth century A.D., Angles and Saxons from Germany came to Britain and settled in separate kingdoms, each with their own king and laws. From the end of eighth century on these kingdoms were attacked by Vikings from Scandinavia.

The Anglo-Saxons, as they became known, arrived in Britain seeking new lands, because their homelands were often flooded by the sea. They fought the Britons to win territory and treasures. King Arthur, a legendary leader of the Britons, is said to have won battles against the invaders at the beginning of the sixth century.

The Lindisfarne Gospels
These pages show the elaborate, decorated initials and designs that introduce the first four books of the New Testament of the Bible, known as the Gospels. They are in the British Museum, London.

The Anglo-Saxons lived in villages of wooden huts with thatched roofs and built wooden forts to defend themselves against enemy attack. They raised animals and farmed the land, using wooden and iron tools. They cremated (burned) their dead and buried the pots of ashes with articles such as weapons and jewelry. One important Anglo-Saxon burial place was found in 1939 at Sutton Hoo in Suffolk, where a king was buried with his ship and all his treasures.

During this period, Christianity was slowly spreading in Britain through the work of missionaries. Monasteries were founded on the islands of Iona in Scotland and Lindisfarne in Northumbria, where monks prayed, studied, and copied out religious works. A very famous example of their painstaking work, the Lindisfarne Gospels (left), was made at Lindisfarne monastery around A.D. 698

Missionaries were sent from Rome by Pope Gregory. They were led by an early Christian leader, Augustine. Augustine converted Anglo-Saxon King Ethelbert to Christianity and became the first Archbishop of Canterbury. More churches were then built throughout the country.

During the late eighth century, Vikings from Scandinavia began to raid the coast of Britain. The first raid was on the monastery of Lindisfarne in A.D. 793. After the 860s, Vikings settled in Britain and soon took over all the Anglo-Saxon kingdoms except Wessex, which was held by King Alfred (849–899). Alfred had a strong army and navy and defeated the Vikings in many battles. After Alfred's death, the Viking attacks began again, and for a time the English crown was held by Danish kings. One of them, King Canute, ruled England from 1016–35. From 1042 England was ruled by the English king, Edward the Confessor. In 1066, however, a Saxon—Harold, Earl of Wessex—laid claim to the throne.

Viking Chessmen
These chess pieces, representing a knight, a queen, and a bishop, were carved from a walrus tusk by a Viking sculptor during the twelfth century. They were found on the Isle of Lewis in Scotland and are now in the British Museum, London.

THE NORMAN CONQUEST

In 1066 Duke William of Normandy sailed from France to claim the English crown. His army defeated King Harold and the Saxons at the Battle of Hastings, and he became William I (the Conqueror) of England.

Duke William of Normandy, who ruled the Normans, also had a claim to the English throne. William was a cousin of King Edward the Confessor, who died without leaving a son to succeed him. William landed his army at Pevensey, in Sussex, while Harold and the Saxons were in the north fighting off a Viking invasion. Harold marched his army south to fight William and his army at the Battle of Hastings. The Normans had a skilled army of horsemen, who fought with the latest battle equipment and followed a clever battle plan. In one day of fierce fighting, Harold was killed (legend says by an arrow through the eye), and the Saxons were defeated.

The story of the Norman Conquest is told in the Bayeux Tapestry, which is embroidered in wool thread on linen panels and measures 231 feet long. The tapestry was made in France about 1080, probably for William's half-brother Odo, who was bishop of Bayeux.

In Norman Britain, society was ordered on a feudal system, where all land was owned by the king or his barons. They were powerful landowners. The serfs, or villagers, served their local lord or baron, working for him in return for land on which they could grow food. The barons served the king and would lead their villagers in battle for him in times of war. A typical Norman village had a church, a few simple huts, and possibly a water mill for grinding corn. After 1066, towns began to grow, often near castles or abbeys.

William the Conqueror ruled until 1087 and was succeeded by his sons. In 1154 his great-grandson, Henry Plantagenet—whose parents owned vast lands in France—became Henry II, the first of the Plantagenet kings.

Rex Interfectus Est—*The King Is Dead*. A scene from the Bayeux Tapestry shows armored knights in battle as King Harold (believed to be the figure on the left) falls to the ground. This work is in the Museum of Queen Matilda, Bayeux, France.

THE MIDDLE AGES

During the period from the sixth to the sixteenth centuries, which is known as the Middle Ages, religion was very important in peoples' lives. Many beautiful cathedrals and abbeys were built during this time. Early in the thirteenth century, conflict between king and barons resulted in the signing of the Magna Carta (Great Charter), which limited the king's powers.

Throughout the Middle Ages, the Christian religion, headed by the pope in Rome, was an important part of everyday life. Parish churches were used for meetings and festivals, as well as for church services. Parish priests took care of the religious affairs of each parish. In most of the larger towns and cities, cathedrals designed in the intricately carved Gothic style were built by masons and craftspeople. They often took many years to complete.

Wells Cathedral
Wells Cathedral in Somerset was built between 1170 and 1370 and was decorated in the early English Gothic style. This is the magnificent west front of the cathedral.

Abbeys and monasteries were very important centers, and the abbots who ran them had great influence. People in the abbeys owned and farmed large areas of land. As well as being centers of Christianity, abbeys and monasteries provided shelter for travelers and care for the sick. They were also important centers of learning. The monks who lived there spent much of their time in prayer and study. A group of monks called friars traveled around the country, preaching and comforting the sick.

The Christian church was very rich and powerful, and bishops competed for power with the king. King Henry II (1133–89) quarreled with the Archbishop of Canterbury, Thomas à Becket. When Becket refused to agree with him, four of the king's knights murdered the archbishop near the altar of Canterbury Cathedral in 1170.

The English kings also quarreled with their barons. King John (1167–1216) became unpopular with the barons because he taxed them heavily to pay for wars against France, during which he lost most of England's French lands. In 1215 the barons met King John at Runnymede meadows, beside the Thames River, and forced him to sign the Magna Carta, a charter (document) that set out their rights and limited the power of the king. The signing of this charter gave the English Parliament more powers than other parliaments of monarchies had at that time.

This picture, made in the Middle Ages, marks the place where St. Thomas à Becket was murdered near the altar of Canterbury Cathedral.

WAR IN FRANCE AND AT HOME

For over a century England and France were at war, as the English kings tried to regain the French lands they had once owned. In 1348 the Black Death spread to England; the plague is estimated to have killed over a third of the population. In the fifteenth century, a civil war, the Wars of the Roses, was fought between rival claimants to the English throne.

◀ Medieval cities were fortified with towers and battlements. In times of trouble people stayed inside the city walls.

For over a hundred years, from 1337 to 1453, England was at war with France over English claims to French lands. During the Hundred Years' War, as it was called, five English kings fought five French kings, winning important victories at Crécy in 1346 and at Agincourt in 1415. In 1429 a young French heroine, Joan of Arc, helped to turn the war in France's favor; and by the time the fighting was over, England retained only the port of Calais on France's northern coast.

In 1348 the Hundred Years' War was interrupted when the Black Death spread to Europe from the East. This terrible disease, which was spread by the fleas carried on rats, killed thousands of people all over Europe. It is estimated that over a third of the population of Europe died from the Black Death.

◀ Pilgrimage to Canterbury

An early sixteenth-century illustration of the English poet John Lydgate (c. 1370–1450) and other pilgrims leaving Canterbury. The illustration is in the British Library, London.

Many pilgrims journeyed to Canterbury to see the place where St. Thomas à Becket was killed.

In 1455 a civil war broke out in England. Battles raged between the armies of two rival houses (families), who both claimed the English throne. The war was called the Wars of the Roses, because it was fought between the House of Lancaster, who chose a red rose as one of their emblems, and the House of York, whose emblem was mistakenly thought to be a white rose. The fighting finally ended in 1485 at the Battle of Bosworth, when Henry Tudor of the House of Lancaster beat King Richard III of York. Henry became king and the Tudor age began.

THE TUDORS

The Tudors ruled England from 1485 to 1603. Although the years of war had ended, there was religious upheaval throughout the country. The Church of England broke away from the authority of the pope. Towns and ports continued to grow as new sea routes opened to overseas lands and trade expanded.

When Henry VII (1457–1509) came to the throne, he wanted to bring peace and order and encourage foreign trade . He still had many enemies, including followers of Richard III, so he married Elizabeth of York to unite the opposing families of Lancaster and York. He built up his wealth and became a powerful king.

When Henry VII died he was succeeded by his son Henry VIII (1491–1547). Henry VIII was a commanding and powerful leader. He appointed famous German artist Hans Holbein the Younger as Court Painter. Holbein painted several magnificent portraits of the king and of his friends and family. Henry married six wives and was inclined to order anyone who displeased him—including his wives and advisers—to be beheaded.

Henry ruled with the help of his powerful chief minister Cardinal Thomas Wolsey. Henry built up a strong army and navy, and he used his military strength to try to seize power in Scotland (which was ruled by the Stuarts) and France, but without success. Above all, Henry wanted a son to succeed him.

When Henry's first wife, a Spanish princess named Catherine of Aragon, failed to give him a son, he divorced her and married an English noblewoman, Anne Boleyn. Anne gave him a daughter, Elizabeth, but no son. Henry accused her of being unfaithful and had her beheaded. He went on to have four more wives, but by the time he died

▲ The king's garter bears the Latin motto of the Order of the Garter, the highest order of knighthood.

A Portrait of Henry VIII
by the court painter Hans Holbein the Younger. This portrait hangs in Belvoir Castle, Leicestershire.

he had only one son, Edward, by his third wife Jane Seymour. In the meantime, by divorcing Catherine of Aragon and marrying Anne Boleyn, Henry had disobeyed the pope in Rome.

THE REFORMATION AND THE DISSOLUTION OF THE MONASTERIES

Henry VIII's break from the Pope was part of a wider religious change taking place in Europe. Dissatisfaction with the way the Roman Catholic Church was being run led to a revolt against the authority of the church. This was known as the Reformation.

▼ In this detail from the painting opposite, the Catholic bishop is shown as a wolf. The dead sheep he wears around his neck represents a bishop who has been put to death for trying to reform the church.

As head of the church, the Pope had refused to allow Henry VIII to divorce his first wife. So, in 1534 Henry broke away from Rome and declared himself Supreme Head of the new Church of England.

As head of the new church, Henry asked his Chancellor, Thomas Cromwell, to make a survey of all the monasteries in England, claiming that the abbots were lazy and corrupt and that the monasteries were poorly run. Henry ordered Cromwell to send men to destroy the monastery buildings and seize all their land and treasures. This was known as the Dissolution of the Monasteries.

When Henry died in 1547, his son, Edward VI, was only nine years old. Edward VI became king, but Edward Seymour, the Duke of Somerset, was named his protector and carried out the king's duties. Edward VI was a strong believer in the new Protestant religion, which was spreading in Europe through the teachings of German monk Martin Luther (1483–1546) and French preacher John Calvin (1509–64). These men wanted church services to be simpler and Christianity to follow more closely the teachings of Christ. When Edward VI died in 1553—at the age of 16—he named Lady Jane Grey, a great-granddaughter of Henry VII, as his successor.

However, after only nine days as queen, Lady Jane Grey, a Protestant. was imprisoned by Roman Catholic enemies and beheaded. Mary Tudor, Henry VIII's eldest daughter, became queen. She was determined to return England to the Catholic Church. She married Philip II, the Catholic heir to the Spanish throne. She also imprisoned and executed leading Protestants, burning hundreds of people at the stake. There was growing unrest at Mary's actions, and many people were happy in 1558 when they heard she had died and England had a new young queen, Elizabeth I.

THE ELIZABETHAN AGE

Elizabeth I (1533–1603) was a strong, intelligent ruler. During her reign, England grew as an industrial and trading power. English explorers sailed across the Atlantic, searching for new lands in which to settle and with which to establish trading links.

During the Elizabethan age, London, Bristol, Liverpool, and other seaports grew quickly with the expansion of trade. Throughout the period, explorers searched for new lands where England could set up colonies and trading links. Sir Walter Raleigh (1552–1618) made several expeditions to the American continent. There were also opportunities for the captains of private warships to seize treasures from Spanish ships returning from America and the Pacific. The most famous of these privateers was Sir Francis Drake (1540–96), who in the 1570s became the first Englishman to sail around the world.

At home, many towns were growing with the development of the cloth industry. Coal mining became more efficient with the introduction of horse-drawn pumps that drained water out of the mines. Coal was used for fuel and in the manufacture of iron, bricks, and glass. Many houses of the period had glass in the windows and were built of wooden frames filled in with brick. Fire was always a risk, especially in the narrow city streets.

◀ This musician is playing a type of cello.

People who broke the law had to appear before justices of the peace, and local constables, called beadles, kept law and order in the towns. People could be hanged for very minor crimes. There were no drainage or sewage systems to get rid of waste and many people suffered from diseases.

Literature and drama flourished. Edmund Spenser (c.1552–99) wrote the poem *The Faerie Queene*, and William Shakespeare (1564–1616) began writing plays during Elizabeth's reign. The first public theaters opened in London, and groups of traveling actors performed in streets and courtyards of inns. Shakespeare's company acted at the Globe Theater, which was built in 1599.

Queen Elizabeth dancing with Robert Dudley, the Earl of Leicester by Marcus Gheeraerts the Younger (c. 1561–1636). Dudley was one of the Queen's favorites. The painting is in a private collection.

The artist was one of a group of Protestant refugees who had come to England to escape the fighting between Catholics and Protestants in France.

QUEEN ELIZABETH AND THE SPANISH ARMADA

In 1588 King Philip II of Spain sent a huge fleet of ships called the Spanish Armada to attack England. Spain, a Catholic country, had been greatly angered by the execution of Mary, Queen of Scots, a Catholic, on Queen Elizabeth's orders. Spain had been infuriated by the raids of the British privateers.

Mary Stuart, Queen of Scots (1542–87), was Elizabeth's cousin. Many Catholics in England wanted Mary to be their queen too, but in Scotland she met with opposition from the growing number of Protestants. Mary became more unpopular with the Scottish people when she was suspected of having her second husband murdered, and she fled to England. Elizabeth knew that Mary was a danger to the throne because many Catholics in England and abroad wanted to make her queen. At first Mary was kept in prison, but after the discovery of a Catholic plot in 1587, Elizabeth was persuaded to have her executed.

The Execution of Mary Queen of Scots by an unknown artist.

Mary is shown holding up a crucifix as the ax falls. The picture is in the Scottish National Gallery, Edinburgh.

This act angered the Catholic King Philip II of Spain. He planned to invade England and take the throne from Elizabeth. An armada of 130 warships set out from Spain in May 1588, but they met heavy storms at sea and lost much of their supplies. When the Spanish ships neared Plymouth, they were attacked by the English fleet and sailed on to Calais where they dropped anchor. The English sent fireships, loaded with explosives, after them.

The Spanish panicked and set sail, opening themselves up to attack by the English ships, which were faster, moved more easily, and had guns that could fire at longer range. After a fierce battle, the Armada was forced to retreat, sailing north around the coasts of Scotland and Ireland to return home to Spain. The ships met more storms, and only about 60 of the original fleet returned safely to Spain.

Queen Elizabeth's navy had won a great victory and had prevented a foreign invasion. By the time she died in 1603, England had become a strong power in Europe. Elizabeth never married, and she named Mary Stuart's son, James VI of Scotland (a Protestant), to succeed her.

The Defeat of the Spanish Armada by an unknown artist. The painting is in the National Maritime Museum, London.

JAMES I—THE FIRST STUART KING

James VI of Scotland (1566–1625) became James I of England in 1603. Although he was not a popular ruler, his reign saw the expansion of British colonies overseas, progress in medicine and science, and the publication of Shakespeare's greatest plays.

Towns in England continued to grow through trade and industries, such as metalworking in Birmingham and Sheffield and cloth making in Manchester and Leeds. The population of London had reached over half a million.

Scientists were making important discoveries. William Harvey (1578–1657) discovered the circulation of the blood, and Francis Bacon (1561–1626) developed a more exact approach to science, based on measurement, observation, and experiment. The arts flourished with the plays of William Shakespeare and Ben Jonson (c. 1573–1637) and a new translation of the Bible.

Religious troubles continued. In 1605 a group of Catholics plotted to blow up the Houses of Parliament in London.

The plot's technical expert was Guido (Guy) Fawkes, who had served with the Spanish army in the Netherlands and knew about explosives. The plotters smuggled barrels of gunpowder into the cellars beneath the Parliament buildings. However, one of the group warned a friend to stay away from Parliament on the scheduled day (November 5), and the plan was discovered. The plotters were rounded up and tortured before being hanged. Their heads were displayed on poles as a warning to others.

There were deep divisions among Catholics, Protestants, and some strict Protestants called Puritans, who wanted to "purify" the Church of England of all Catholic influences. In 1620 a group of Puritans set sail from Plymouth, in Devon, for the Americas, to seek a new life and the freedom to worship as they wished. The Pilgrims, as they became known, reached the coast of North America, where they founded Plymouth Colony in the present-day state of Massachusetts.

Guy Fawkes before King James
by nineteenth-century artist
Sir John Gilbert (1817–97).

This painting shows Guy Fawkes (kneeling) being brought to trial before King James I. It is owned by Harrogate Museums and Art Gallery.

THE CIVIL WAR

The second Stuart king was James I's son, Charles I (1600–49). Religious and political quarrels between the king and Parliament plunged England into civil war (1642-46). The war was fought between the Royalists (or Cavaliers), supporters of Charles I, and the Roundheads (called so because they cut their hair short), supporters of Parliament.

By the beginning of Charles's reign, the Puritan religion was becoming stronger among Members of Parliament (MPs) and throughout the country. Parliament disliked the fact that Charles had married a French Catholic princess and resented the heavy taxes the king was charging to pay for wars in Europe. When MPs tried to limit the king's power, he imprisoned the leaders and dismissed Parliament. For eleven years Charles ruled without Parliament.

When Parliament was recalled in 1640, the members again tried to limit the king's power. Charles tried to arrest the leaders, but they escaped and rallied support outside London. In 1642 Charles marched his army to Nottingham and fought the parliamentary forces at the Battle of Edgehill. The country was now divided, with the south and east siding mainly with Parliament and the north and west fighting for the king. Catholics, lords, and the wealthy were mostly royalists; Puritans, members of the House of Commons, and working people fought for Parliament.

King Charles's head was cut off with ▶ one blow and held up by the executioner for the crowds to see.

The first important battle was won by parliamentary troops at Marston Moor in Yorkshire (1644). The leader of the parliamentary forces, Oliver Cromwell (1599–1658), built up a skilled professional army, and his soldiers went on to win decisive battles at Naseby and Langport in 1645. The king surrendered and was charged with treason against Parliament and the country. On January 30, 1649, he was publicly beheaded in London.

Cromwell then declared himself Lord Protector of a united Commonwealth of England, Scotland, Ireland, and the colonies. The Protectorate was a period of strict Puritanism. Theaters were closed, dancing was forbidden, and Catholic churches were stripped of their treasures. By 1658, when Cromwell died, the country was looking for new leadership and a new beginning.

The Execution of King Charles I at Whitehall on January 30, 1649 by Gonzales Coques (c. 1614–84), who was born in the Netherlands and lived in London for a time.

Charles, shown on the left with his crown fallen, said, "I fear not death. I bless my God I am prepared." The painting is in the Museum of Picardy, in Amiens, France.

RESTORATION AND REVOLUTION

In 1660 Charles II (1630–85), the eldest son of the beheaded Charles I, was given the throne. In 1688, following the "Glorious Revolution," his successor James II (a Catholic) was forced to leave Britain. The Dutch Protestant Prince William of Orange and his wife Mary (daughter of James II) were invited to take the throne.

Coronation Procession of Charles II from Westminster to the Tower of London
by Dutch artist Dirck Stoop (c. 1618–86). This painting is in the Museum of London.

In 1660 Parliament recalled Charles II from exile, and the monarchy was restored. The citizens of Britain were tired of the dull life that they had lived under Oliver Cromwell, and they rejoiced when Charles II was crowned king.

The Restoration period brought progress in many fields. In 1662 the Royal Society was set up to promote the study of science, with members including the great scientist Sir Isaac Newton (1642–1727). Overseas, the British Empire expanded as new colonies were settled in North America and trading stations were established in the Far East by the East India Company.

In London, overcrowded buildings and the lack of decent drains led to an outbreak of a plague in 1665. The following year, on September 2, a fire broke out in a baker's shop on Pudding Lane, spreading rapidly through the timber-framed houses and destroying much of the city.

Charles II died in 1685. His successor, his brother James II (1633–1701), was a Catholic. The Duke of Monmouth, Charles II's illegitimate son, attempted to take the throne from James, but failed. Monmouth landed in Dorset and fought the Battle of Sedgemoor in 1685, but he and his followers were defeated, rounded up, and executed.

James remained king but Parliament disliked the fact that he kept a large army and gave important jobs to Catholics. In 1688 he fled to France after Parliament invited his Protestant daughter Mary and her husband, Prince William of Orange, to take the English throne. William and Mary ruled until 1702, when Mary's sister Anne (1665–1714) succeeded. It was during Anne's reign that the Parliaments of England and Scotland were joined under the Union Jack flag by the Act of Union of 1707.

The Fire of London, 1666
An unknown seventeenth-century English artist painted this dramatic scene of the fire, which burned for four days and destroyed 87 churches and more than 13,000 homes. The painting is in the Guildhall Art Gallery, London.

Architect Sir Christopher Wren (1002–1723) drew up plans for rebuilding the city with wider streets and brick houses. He also designed new churches, including St. Paul's Cathedral, the largest cathedral in England.

THE INDUSTRIAL REVOLUTION

During the eighteenth century, Britain changed from being a mainly agricultural country to become an important industrial power. New inventions revolutionized manufacturing, transportation, and communication.

Morning at Coalbrookdale, 1777 by William Williams (1727-91). The smoking chimneys of the factories are a sign of the new industrial age. This painting is in Clive House Museum, Shrewsbury.

For centuries, most people in Britain had lived in the countryside and farmed the land or worked in their own homes at crafts such as carpentry, spinning, or weaving. By the eighteenth century, huge changes were taking place. In 1733 the invention of a faster loom, the Flying Shuttle, made weaving much quicker.

Traditional spinning wheels could not keep up the supply of yarn needed for the faster weaving methods. In 1764, James Hargreaves invented the more efficient Spinning Jenny, and five years later Richard Arkwright (1732–92) invented a water-powered spinning machine that could do the work of 12 people. Factories and mills using the new machines began to spring up, and gradually more people went out to work instead of working in their own homes.

In 1775 James Watt (1736–1819) adapted and improved the steam engine, first invented by Thomas Newcomen in 1712. This machine was used to pump water out of coal mines to prevent flooding. Coal was used for the manufacture of iron and for other industries, and manufacturing towns began to grow up close to the coal mines of the Midlands and the north country. In 1781 Watt built a steam engine that could drive factory machinery.

As industry grew, transportation and communication also improved. A network of canals was built so that goods could be transported by water. Roads were improved, and tollgates were introduced to help pay for the roads. John McAdam (1756–1836), a Scot, invented a new road surface that made traveling smoother and more comfortable. Regular coaches ran between London and other major towns, stopping at various points, called stages, to pick up or drop off passengers and change horses.

THE GEORGIAN AGE

Queen Anne, the last Stuart monarch, died in 1714. Although she had many children, none lived to adulthood. So the British crown passed to Protestant descendants of James I, who belonged to the German House of Hanover. The Georgian age that followed is famous for the style and elegance of its art and architecture, landscape gardening, and furniture.

Parliament chose a Hanoverian king to prevent a Catholic king or queen from succeeding to the British throne. But there were two attempts by the Stuarts to retake the throne, supported by discontented Catholics. In 1715 the Scots supported an uprising led by James II's son, James Edward (known as the Old Pretender). The uprising was defeated, but in 1745 his son Charles Edward or Bonnie Prince Charlie (the Young Pretender) sailed from France to Scotland, where he rallied support among the Highland chiefs. He led his army south as far as Derby before he was forced to retreat. The army was defeated at the Battle of Culloden in 1746.

The new king, George I (1660–1727), spoke no English and ruled with the help of his ministers, especially Robert Walpole, who became Britain's first prime minister.

Stourhead Gardens
These landscaped gardens in Wiltshire were begun in 1741. They were laid out in the classical style and were adorned with temples, grottoes, and statues.

Mr. and Mrs. Andrews
by Thomas Gainsborough
(1727–88). This painting is in the
National Gallery, London.

In the eighteenth century it was
considered fashionable to have
one's portrait painted in landscape
settings. Here Gainsborough has
painted a wealthy landowner and
his wife against the setting of their
country estate.

Walpole helped Britain recover from the financial crash of
the South Sea Trading Company, known as the South Sea
Bubble (in 1720) and worked to build up the country's
wealth and trade.

For the rich, there were many new pleasures in the
Georgian age. New country houses were built, with
grounds laid out as landscaped parks following the
fashion created by Lancelot "Capability" Brown (1716–83).
The arts flourished, including fine furniture by designers
such as Chippendale and Hepplewhite, pottery from the
factories of Josiah Wedgwood, and drama and literature—
including a new art form, the novel. The works of artists
such as William Hogarth (1697–1764), Joshua Reynolds
(1723–92), and Thomas Gainsborough (1727–88) were in
great demand.

33

WAR OVERSEAS

Britain's colonies and overseas trade continued to expand during the eighteenth century; but in America, the colonists were ready for independence. At home, Britain faced the threat of a French invasion, led by Emperor Napoleon Bonaparte.

By the mid-eighteenth century, two million British settlers were living in North America. They still had to pay taxes to the British government and all their goods had to pass through Britain. The settlers were unhappy with this situation and, in 1770, there were riots in Boston. The British government canceled all taxes except the tax on tea. On December 16, 1773, an East India Company ship docked at Boston with a shipment of tea. A group of colonists disguised as Native Americans managed to get on board. They seized the tea crates and threw them into the harbor. The British government demanded payment and threatened to close the port, but the colonists began arming themselves and preparing for war.

Under the leadership of George Washington, many colonists formed a professional army. By 1778, when the French joined the fight on the American side, the war began to turn against the British. On October 17, 1781, Britain surrendered. America was now an independent country.

The Surrender of General Burgoyne at Saratoga
by John Trumbull (1756–1843). This painting is in the Trumbull Gallery at Yale University, New Haven, Connecticut.

The American victory at this battle, fought in October 1777, was a turning point in the war against Britain.

In 1805 Britain faced the threat of invasion by the French. Emperor Napoleon Bonaparte sent warships into the English Channel, but they were defeated at the battle of Trafalgar by the British navy under Admiral Horatio Nelson, who died in the fighting. In 1808 Napoleon's armies occupied Spain. The British sent troops to help the Spanish, and by 1814 they were gaining ground and invaded France. Napoleon gave up the throne and was sent to the island of Elba in the Mediterranean. A hundred days later he escaped, and in 1815 he fought his last great battle, at Waterloo in Belgium. The French were defeated by British forces led by the Duke of Wellington and Prussian troops. Napoleon was imprisoned on the island of St. Helena, where he died in 1821.

The Death of Nelson
by Denis Dighton (1792–1827). This painting is in the National Maritime Museum, London.

Admiral Nelson was killed at the Battle of Trafalgar in 1805. He died on the lowest deck of H.M.S. *Victory*, and his body was taken back to London, preserved in a cask of brandy. His tragic death gripped the imagination of the British people, and many pictures were painted of the event.

VICTORIAN BRITAIN

Queen Victoria reigned from 1837–1901. During her reign, trade and communications improved and industry expanded. By the 1890s, the British Empire was at the height of its power, ruling Australia, Canada, New Zealand, large parts of Africa, the Indian subcontinent, and colonies all over the world.

The Victorian age brought many changes. For the wealthy upper and middle classes, homes became much more comfortable and were equipped with hot water systems, gas lighting, and bathrooms.

Throughout Victoria's reign great improvements were made in communications. The postal service was introduced, with the Penny Post carrying letters any distance for the cost of one penny for every half ounce in weight. Communications opened up even more with the later inventions of the telegraph system (passing messages along electrical wire) and the telephone.

The invention of the railroad made travel faster, easier, and available to more people. In towns, traffic increased with trolleys running alongside horse-drawn omnibuses, hansom cabs, and bicycles. In London the world's first subway opened in 1863. Steamships replaced sailing ships, and wooden hulls were replaced with iron.

The little girl on her mother's knee has a toy drum and bugle to play with on the journey. ▼

There were also important political reforms. Many children, as young as eight years old, worked long hours in factories and mines. Reforms were gradually introduced, limiting a child's workday to eight hours and preventing women or children from working in mines. The Reform Act of 1867 gave working men in towns the right to vote. The Education Act of 1870 introduced the first state schools, providing education for all children between the ages of five and thirteen.

For those who could not find work and who were reduced to begging on the streets, the only escape was the workhouse, where living and working conditions were very hard. Many people sought a new life by emigrating to the United States or to one of the countries in Britain's huge overseas empire.

Omnibus Life in London
by William Maw Egley (1826–1916). This vivid scene shows passengers in a horse-drawn omnibus. It is in the Tate Gallery, London.

THE EDWARDIANS

The twentieth century began with the Edwardian age. This was a period of peace and stability, and Britain was the head of a vast and powerful empire. But at home there were deep divisions between rich and poor. New inventions were changing people's home and working lives.

Queen Victoria died in 1901, and the new century began with Edward VII (1841–1910) as king. The first automobiles appeared on the roads and were soon replacing horse-drawn carriages. Electric lighting and telephones were becoming more widely available, although it was only the wealthy who could afford them. Movie theaters opened in the larger towns, showing silent movies that were enjoyed by many people. But almost one third of the population still lived in real hardship and poverty.

Between 1905 and the outbreak of World War I in 1914, the Liberal government passed several Acts of Parliament in an attempt to improve the lives of the poor.

In 1906 free school meals were introduced. The following year David Lloyd George, as Chancellor of the Exchequer, drew up a plan to pay pensions to the elderly. This came into force in 1909. In 1911 the National Insurance bill introduced insurance payments for the sick and the unemployed.

Women were still not allowed to vote in general elections. In 1903 Emmeline Pankhurst set up the Women's Social and Political Union. Her members were called Suffragettes because they campaigned for women's suffrage (the right to vote in elections). They chained themselves to railings, went on hunger strikes, damaged public property, and demonstrated in the streets, but they had to wait until until after World War I before they were able to vote.

Torturing Women in Prison ▶
– Vote Against the Government
The suffragettes produced propaganda posters to spread their message. This poster was published by the National Women's Social and Political Union. It is in the British Library, London.

The efforts of Emmeline Pankhurst and the Suffragettes often landed the women in prison. Sometimes they would protest by refusing to eat and would be forcibly fed by prison staff.

1913
TORTURING WOMEN IN PRISON
E R
Votes for Women
PUBLISHED BY THE NATIONAL WOMEN'S SOCIAL AND POLITICAL UNION 4 CLEMENTS INN STRAND W.C. & PRINTED BY DAVID ALLEN & SONS LD 180 FLEET ST E.C.
VOTE AGAINST THE GOVERNMENT

WORLD WAR I

In 1914, the assassination of Archduke Ferdinand, the heir to the Austro-Hungarian Empire, triggered World War I, bringing four years of bloodshed and resulting in lasting changes to British society.

Returning to the Trenches
by C. R. W. Nevinson (1899–1946).
The painting is in the National
Gallery of Canada, Ottawa, Ontario.

The artist has captured the bleak
trench landscape of northern
France, illuminated by an exploding
star shell.

On June 28, 1914, while visiting Sarajevo in Bosnia, Archduke Ferdinand of Austria and his wife were killed by a Serbian student. The student wanted Serbia to be independent of the Austro-Hungarian empire. His action resulted in the invasion of Serbia by Austrian armies; they were backed by Germany, which had become a very powerful nation. In 1914 German troops invaded Belgium, which was not involved in the war, and marched into northern France.

Britain joined with France and Russia against Germany and Austria. Most people believed the war would end quickly but the opposing armies became deadlocked in battle. They fought from deep, muddy trenches that stretched from the Channel coast to the French border with Switzerland. Hundreds of thousands of soldiers died in the fierce battles of Verdun and the Somme River.

In 1917 the United States joined Britain and her allies; the following year the Allied armies finally drove the Germans back across their borders. The Germans signed an armistice (truce), and the Great War was over.

Many changes followed. Women, who had performed important jobs while the men were away fighting, were finally allowed to vote. Those over 30 were allowed to vote in 1918; by 1928, women 21 and older could vote. There were more cars on the roads, and many houses now had wireless sets (radios). More movie theaters opened, and "talkies" began to replace silent films in 1929. Many people could not afford any kind of luxury because there was high unemployment. In 1926 a strike by coal miners, protesting pay cuts, triggered the General Strike, when workers all over the country stopped working. The strike failed, and workers everywhere felt let down by the government.

DEPRESSION AND WAR

The 1930s were a time of worldwide economic depression. In Germany a new government came to power under Adolf Hitler, who was determined to win back land lost in World War I. When German troops invaded Poland in 1939, Britain and her ally France declared war on Germany. This was the start of World War II.

For many British people, the 1930s were a time of great hardship. Large numbers were out of work, and there was a feeling of uneasiness in the country. Many people felt unsettled when, in 1936 King Edward VIII gave up the throne to marry an American divorcée, Mrs. Wallis Simpson. Edward's brother George VI succeeded to the throne.

There was a growing fear of war as Hitler rearmed Germany and made plans to expand German lands in Europe. In 1938 the Germans occupied Austria and Czechoslovakia, and the following year they invaded Poland. In September 1939 Britain declared war on Germany and sent troops to defend France. By May 1940 the Germans had marched through Belgium into France, trapping the British soldiers on the coast at Dunkirk. The British sent every ship and boat available to rescue the troops and bring them home.

Hitler planned to invade Britain and sent planes to attack British air power. Royal Air Force fighter planes repelled them, battling with the German planes in the skies above southern England as Paul Nash's painting so clearly shows. These ferocious aerial fights, which took place in the late summer of 1940, came to be called the Battle of Britain by Winston Churchill, Britain's prime minister and war leader. The Germans then began bombing British cities. Many people were killed or lost their homes and belongings in the air raids. There were shortages of food, clothing, and gasoline, and rationing was introduced.

The war spread to Africa and the Far East. In 1941, after Japanese war planes destroyed the U.S. naval base at Pearl Harbor in the Pacific, Britain and the United States declared war on Japan. On D day, June 6, 1944, the allies landed on the beaches of Normandy in France. As the allied armies swept inland, Hitler committed suicide on April 30, 1945, and Germany surrendered on May 7. The war in Europe was over. Three months later the war in the Far East ended after the United States dropped atomic bombs that devastated the Japanese cities of Hiroshima and Nagasaki.

The Battle of Britain, August to October 1940 by Paul Nash (1889–1946), is in the Imperial War Museum, London.
Nash was one of Britain's official war artists. Here he captures the drama of the Battle of Britain. The swirling shapes created by the vapor trails of the aircraft mimic the curves of the river below.

POSTWAR BRITAIN

The postwar years brought lasting changes to people's lives. From the 1950s on, many people in Britain began to enjoy a higher standard of living than ever before. But toward the end of the twentieth century unemployment climbed again, as technology brought more changes to society.

A Panoramic View of London in five panels by Ceri Richards (1903–71), is in a private collection. The artist has mapped out London's famous landmarks. On the left is St. Paul's Cathedral, standing alone, without the tall office buildings that now surround it.

After the war the Labour Party came to power. They introduced the National Health Service to provide free health care for all. Gradually peacetime industry revived; London and other cities destroyed by German bombs were rebuilt, and the economy recovered from the war. In 1952 George VI died and Elizabeth II became queen. For the first time, many people were able to watch a coronation on television.

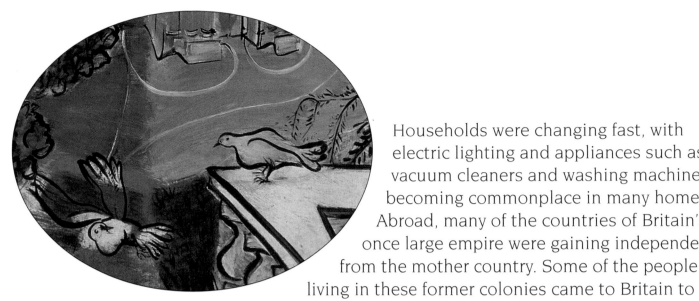

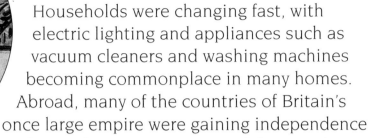

Households were changing fast, with electric lighting and appliances such as vacuum cleaners and washing machines becoming commonplace in many homes. Abroad, many of the countries of Britain's once large empire were gaining independence from the mother country. Some of the people living in these former colonies came to Britain to find work, settling mainly in the larger industrial cities.

▲ On this sunny day the London pigeons might remind the viewer of doves of peace.

The 1960s were a boom time for Britain. London became world famous for fashion design, and rock groups such as the Beatles introduced a new kind of music. In 1965 natural gas was discovered in the North Sea, and in 1973 Britain joined the European Economic Community (now known as the European Union, or EU). Manufacturing industries were declining, however, with coal mines, steelworks, shipyards, and factories closing down, leading to many job losses. Service industries such as tourism and banking increased in importance, and London became an international business center.

Britain has faced many problems in the last decades of the twentieth century. In 1982 a war with Argentina was fought and won, to keep the far-off colony of the Falkland Islands British. Troubles in Northern Ireland, started when British troops were sent there in 1969 to try to keep peace between Catholic Republicans and Protestant Loyalists, have continued. Unemployment and homelessness remain high, even though, as the century closes, many people in Britain today enjoy a higher standard of living than ever before.

GLOSSARY

allegory A picture or story that has a second meaning or message.

allies Nations joining together for a common purpose.

assassination The murder of an important person.

barbarian Primitive or uncivilized.

barons Noblemen who leased land from the king in the Middle Ages.

Christianity The religion based on the teachings of Jesus Christ.

civil war A war between citizens of one country.

colonies Settlements of people, called colonists, who have moved to live in another country.

East India Company The trading company set up by the British government in 1600.

economic depression A poor period, with high unemployment, in the economy of a nation.

emigrating Leaving one's own country to settle in another.

empire A group of countries or states under one ruler.

feudal Relating to the legal and social system that developed in Europe in the eighth and ninth centuries.

heir The person who legally succeeds to the throne after the death of a king or queen.

invasion The entering of another country in order to take it over.

legendary Of or relating to legend, a popular story handed down from earlier times.

missionaries People who go to foreign countries to teach their religious beliefs.

monarchy A kingdom or government ruled by a king or queen.

parish A district with its own church and clergy.

Parliament A council of state, similar to the United States Congress. In Britain it is divided between the House of Commons (the lower house) and the House of Lords (upper house).

pilgrims People who travel to a holy place as a religious act.

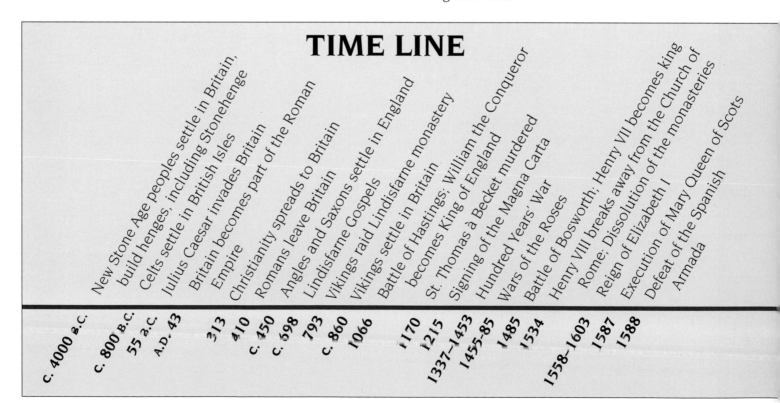

TIME LINE

c. 4000 B.C.	New Stone Age peoples settle in Britain, build henges, including Stonehenge
c. 800 B.C.	Celts settle in British Isles
55 B.C.	Julius Caesar invades Britain
A.D. 43	Britain becomes part of the Roman Empire
313	Christianity spreads to Britain
410	Romans leave Britain
c. 450	Angles and Saxons settle in England
c. 698	Lindisfarne Gospels
793	Vikings raid Lindisfarne monastery
c. 860	Vikings settle in Britain
1066	Battle of Hastings; William the Conqueror becomes King of England
1170	St. Thomas à Becket murdered
1215	Signing of the Magna Carta
1337–1453	Hundred Years' War
1455–85	Wars of the Roses
1485	Battle of Bosworth; Henry VII becomes king
1534	Henry VIII breaks away from the Church of Rome; Dissolution of the monasteries
1558–1603	Reign of Elizabeth I
1587	Execution of Mary Queen of Scots
1588	Defeat of the Spanish Armada

plague An infectious, usually deadly, disease.

Protectorate The period when Oliver Cromwell ruled England as Lord Protector.

Protestant A member of one of the Christian churches that formed as a result of the Reformation.

Prussians People living in Prussia, a large country that is now part of Germany.

Puritans Strict protestants who disapproved of the pleasures of life.

rationing Restricting the amount of food or other goods allowed per person.

reforms Changes and improvements in the law.

Roman Empire The territories ruled by ancient Rome in the first four centuries A.D.

treason Disloyalty to one's country.

wattle and daub Walls made by weaving soft branches together and covering them with clay.

workhouse An institution where very poor people lived and worked.

FURTHER READING

Bush, Catherine. *Elizabeth I*. World Leaders: Past and Present. New York: Chelsea House, 1985.

Dale, Rodney. *The Industrial Revolution*. Discoveries and Inventions. New York: Oxford University Press, 1992.

Denny, Roz. *A Taste of Britain*. Food Around the World. New York: Thomson Learning, 1994.

Janson, H.W. & Janson, Anthony F. *History of Art for Young People*. New York: Harry N. Abrams, 1992.

McHugh, Christopher. *Western Art 1600-1800*. Art and Artists. New York: Thomson Learning, 1994.

Rodgers, Daniel. *The Thames*. Rivers of the World. Milwaukee: Raintree Steck-Vaughn, 1993.

Shearman, Deirdre. *Queen Victoria*. World Leaders: Past and Present. New York: Chelsea House, 1987.

Steele, Philip. *Great Britain*. Discovering. New York: Crestwood House, 1994.

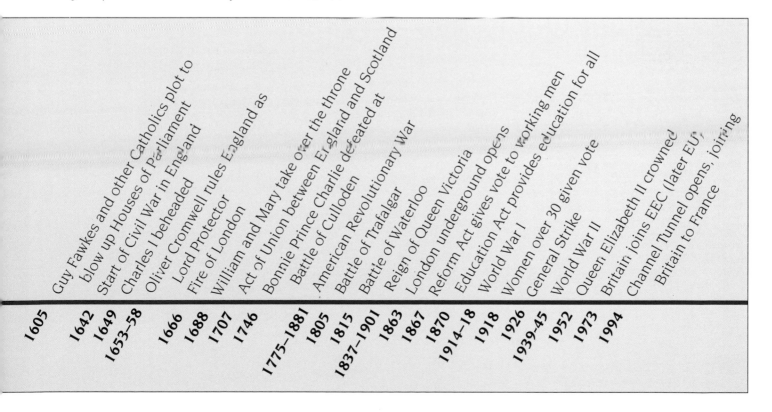

1605 Guy Fawkes and other Catholics plot to blow up Houses of Parliament
1642 Start of Civil War in England
1649 Charles I beheaded
1653–58 Oliver Cromwell rules England as Lord Protector
1666 Fire of London
1688 William and Mary take over the throne
1707 Act of Union between England and Scotland
1746 Bonnie Prince Charlie defeated at Battle of Culloden
1775–1881 American Revolutionary War
1805 Battle of Trafalgar
1815 Battle of Waterloo
1837–1901 Reign of Queen Victoria
1863 London underground opens
1867 Reform Act gives vote to working men
1870 Education Act provides education for all
1914–18 World War I
1918 Women over 30 given vote
1926 General Strike
1939–45 World War II
1952 Queen Elizabeth II crowned
1973 Britain joins EEC (later EU)
1994 Channel Tunnel opens, joining Britain to France

INDEX